NATIONAL LEAGUE EAST

THE ATLANTA BRAVES, THE FLORIDA MARLINS, THE NEW YORK METS, THE PHILADELPHIA PHILLIES, AND THE WASHINGTON NATIONALS

Outfield
Hank Aaron

BY MICHAEL TEITELBAUM

National League East: The Atlanta Braves, the Florida Marlins, the New York Mets, the Philadelphia Phillies, and the Washington Nationals

Published in the United States of America by The Child's World®

PO Box 326 • Chanhassen, MN 55317-0326 • 800-599-READ • www.childsworld.com

Acknowledgements:

The Child's World®: Mary Berendes, Publishing Director

Editorial Directions, Inc.: E. Russell Primm, Editorial Director; Matthew Messbarger, Line Editor; Katie Marsico, Assistant Editor; Susan Hindman, Copy Editor; Sarah E. De Capua, Proofreader; Kevin Cunningham, Fact Checker; Tim Griffin/IndexServ, Indexer; James Buckley Jr., Photo Researcher and Selector

The Design Lab: Kathleen Petelinsek, Art Direction and Design; Kari Thornborough, Page Production

Cover:
Jim Thome

Page one:
Hank Aaron

Photos:

AP: 7, 28
Bettmann/Corbis: 21
Jonathan Daniel/Getty: Cover
Eric Draper/AP: 15
Stephen Dunn/Allsport/Getty: 11
Craig Fujii/AP: 39
Harry Harris/AP: 9
Gary Hershorn/AP: 18
Julie Jacobson/AP: 26
Ralph Morse/Time Life Pictures/Getty: 29
National Baseball Hall of Fame/AP: 6, 27
Rich Pilling/MLB/Getty: 12, 20, 22, 30, 32, 36, 38, 40
Francois Roy/AP: 41
Rucker Archives: 1, 4
H. Rumph Jr./AP: 34
Eliot J. Schechter/Getty: 17
Ezra Shaw/Getty: 24

Library of Congress Cataloging-in-Publication Data

Library of Congress Cataloging-in-Publication Data
Teitelbaum, Michael.
   National League East / by Michael Teitelbaum.
      p. cm. — (Behind the plate)
   Includes index.
   ISBN 1-59296-362-5 (library bound : alk. paper) 1. National League of Professional Baseball Clubs—Juvenile literature. 2. Baseball teams—United States—Juvenile literature. I. Title. II. Series.
   GV875.A3T45 2004
   796.357'64'0973—dc22   2004016846

Table of Contents

: Atlanta Braves

ed: 1871

Turner Field

pened: 1997

: Navy blue and
red

Florida Marlins

d: 1993

o Player

ened: 1987

qua, black,

The road that led to the current National League (NL) East began more than 125 years ago. The NL was formed in 1876. After a rocky start, the league stabilized into an eight-team league with an agreed-upon set of rules in 1900, one year before the rival American League (AL) came into being. The NL in 1900 featured clubs in Boston, Brooklyn, Chicago, Cincinnati, New York, Philadelphia, Pittsburgh, and St. Louis. These eight teams would comprise the NL for the next 53 years. Of those original teams, only the Phillies remain in today's NL East.

The NL remained unchanged until 1953, when the Boston Braves moved to Milwaukee. Then in 1958, the Brooklyn Dodgers moved to Los Angeles, and the New York Giants moved to San Francisco, introducing major league baseball to California.

In 1962, the NL expanded to a 10-team league, adding two new clubs: the Houston Colt .45s and the New York Mets. The Mets' arrival in the league marked the return of NL baseball to New York City.

1908 PHILADELPHIA BASE BALL CLUB
NATIONAL LEAGUE.

1—Grant	7—Richie	13—McQuillin
2—Corridon	8—Courtney	14—Moren
3—Titus	9—Osborne	15—Bransfield
4—Magee.	10—Knabe	16—Brown
5—Dooin	11—Gleason	17—Jacklitsch
6—Doolin	12—Sparks	18—Thomas

With its move to the Astrodome, the world's first indoor baseball stadium, the Houston team changed its name to the Astros in 1965. The following year, the Braves moved again, this time to Atlanta, where they still play today in the NL East.

The year 1969 saw a huge change in the league. For the first time ever, the NL was split into two divisions—East and West. That same year, two more teams were added to the NL—the San Diego Padres and the Montreal Expos—bringing the total to 12 teams. An additional round of **postseason** playoffs, known as the League Championship Series, was added in each league to determine which two teams would go to the **World Series.**

In 1969, the NL East was made up of six teams: the Chicago Cubs, the Montreal Expos, the New York Mets, the Philadelphia Phillies, the Pittsburgh Pirates, and the St. Louis Cardinals. The Expos were Canada's first major league baseball team.

A seventh team, the Florida Marlins, was added to the NL East in 1993. The following year, the league reorganized into three divisions—East, West, and Central. The new NL East became a five-team division featuring the Braves, Marlins, Expos, Mets, and Phillies. The lone change since then came following the 2004 season, when the Expos moved from Montreal to Washington, D.C.

Team: New York Mets
Founded: 1962
Park: Shea Stadium
Park Opened: 1964
Colors: Black, blue, and orange

Team: Philadelphia Phillies
Founded: 1883
Park: Citizens Bank Park
Park Opened: 2004
Color: Red

Team: Washington Nationals
Founded: 1969
Park: RFK Stadium
Park Opened: 1962
Colors: Red, white, and blue

The Atlanta Braves

The Atlanta Braves began their life as the Boston Red Stockings (not to be confused with today's Boston Red Sox) in 1871. The franchise enjoyed success in the late 1870s and early 1880s, winning seven **pennants,** three in the NL. Over the next decade, the team—renamed the Boston Beaneaters in 1883—won five more NL pennants. In 1894, Hall of Famer Hugh Duffy batted .440, still the highest single-season batting average in major league history.

As the 20th century dawned, the Beaneaters slumped—a skid that would last for 14 years. In 1911, the team changed its name again, becoming the Braves. In 1914, they stunned the heavily favored Philadelphia Athletics by sweeping them for their first World Series win.

From 1917 to 1945, the Braves experienced the worst streak in

EDWIN LEE MATHEWS
BOSTON N.L., MILWAUKEE N.L.,
ATLANTA N.L., HOUSTON N.L.,
DETROIT A.L., 1952-1968
BECAME SEVENTH PLAYER IN MAJOR LEAGUE
HISTORY TO HIT 500 HOME RUNS. FINISHED
CAREER WITH 512. HIT 30 OR MORE HOMERS
NINE YEARS IN ROW, 1953-1961, REACHING
40 MARK FOUR TIMES. ESTABLISHED RECORD
FOR HOMERS IN SEASON BY THIRD BASEMAN
WITH 47 IN 1953. LED N.L. IN HOME RUNS
TWICE AND IN WALKS FOUR TIMES. HAD FIVE
SEASONS OF 100 OR MORE RUNS BATTED IN.

"Spahn and Sain and pray for rain" was the famous saying of Braves fans in 1948. The pitching aces (Warren Spahn, left, and Johnny Sain) led the club to the NL pennant.

their history, annually finishing in or near the **cellar.** Then in 1948, pitching stars Warren Spahn and Johnny Sain led the Braves to win their first pennant since 1914. But the team ultimately lost to Cleveland in the World Series.

By 1952, the Braves had fallen to seventh place, and attendance in Boston had dropped greatly. Owner Lou Perini moved the club to Milwaukee

In the first game in NL history in 1876, the Braves (then in Boston) scored twice in the top of the ninth inning to beat the Philadelphia Athletics 6–5.

As Hank Aaron approached Babe Ruth's all-time home run record in 1973, a huge amount of pressure and media attention surrounded the Braves star. Hate mail poured in from people who did not want an African American to break Babe Ruth's mark. When word of the hate mail got out, thousands of letters of support came pouring in—many from children. Aaron broke Ruth's record on April 8, 1974, when he smacked homer number 715.

after the 1952 season, marking the first change in the NL's setup since 1900.

Attendance in Milwaukee soared. The team bounced back, too, finishing second in 1953. The Braves boasted the league's best pitching staff, led by Spahn, second-year pitcher Lew Burdette, and rookie Bob Buhl. Third baseman Eddie Mathews led the league in home runs.

In 1954, Hank Aaron, a star in the fading **Negro Leagues,** joined the Braves. In his 23-year big-league career (his first 21 seasons were with the Braves), he became the game's all-time leading home run hitter. In 1957, the Braves won the NL pennant by eight games, then beat the powerful Yankees in seven games in the World Series for their first champion- ship since 1914.

The Braves won the pennant again the next year, but lost to the Yankees in the World Series. As the Braves fell from the top of the NL standings, attendance started to plummet. By 1965, attendance reached an all-time low. So the Braves moved again, this time to Atlanta, where they remain today.

In 1969, the NL split into two divisions—East and West. The Braves were placed in the West.

With this swing, Hank Aaron became baseball's all-time home run leader.

There they won their division, only to be swept
by the "Miracle" New York Mets in the first NL
Championship Series (NLCS).

Though by then Hank Aaron had blossomed into
a full-blown superstar, the 1970s were lean years
for the team. After breaking Babe Ruth's all-time

For 50 years since his debut in 1954, Hank Aaron's name came first alphabetically on the big league's all-time list of players. In 2004, though, he was displaced at the top by David Aardsma, a rookie pitcher for the San Francisco Giants.

In 2003, Atlanta pitcher Greg Maddux set a big-league record when he posted his 16th consecutive season of 15 or more wins.

home run record in 1974, Aaron left the Braves. He returned to Milwaukee in 1975 to play for the AL's Brewers.

The Braves' next success came in 1982, when they won the West—led by slugger Dale Murphy and **veteran** pitcher Phil Niekro. By 1990, however, the Braves had sunk to last place in the division.

The following year, Atlanta staged a "worst-to-first" comeback. They captured the NL West, then won their first pennant in Atlanta, beating the Pirates in the NLCS. The 1991 Braves were led by a trio of young pitchers—Tom Glavine, Steve Avery, and John Smoltz—who would dominate the NL for years to come. Terry Pendleton, David Justice, and Ron Gant provided the offense. In the '91 World Series against the Minnesota Twins, the Braves lost a closely fought seven-game series.

The Braves became *the* NL team of the '90s—at least based on their performance during the regular season. In 1992 and '93, they took the NL West again, losing in the NLCS in 1993.

In 1994, the league reorganized into three divisions, and the Braves moved into the NL East. The following season, Atlanta won the NL East, and later beat Colorado and Cincinnati for the pennant. Then the Braves edged Cleveland to win their only World Series of the 1990s.

Pitcher Greg Maddux joined the Braves' strong staff in 1993. In 1995, Maddux won his record fourth **Cy Young Award** in a row. Rookie Chipper Jones led the way offensively.

Former Braves star Warren Spahn hit more career home runs (35) than any other pitcher in NL history.

John Smoltz evolved from a dominant starter to one of the best closers in the game.

In 1996, Atlanta won the NL East again. This time, it was John Smoltz who captured the Cy Young Award. The Braves went on to win the East each year after that through 2004. It was the longest division-championship streak ever in baseball. The Braves were clearly the dominant team in the NL in the '90s, but they could not manage another World Series championship.

After being traded from St. Louis, outfielder J. D. Drew had a breakthrough season in 2004.

The Florida Marlins

In 1993, the NL expanded for the first time since 1969. Teams were added in Denver (the Colorado Rockies joined the NL West) and in Miami (the Florida Marlins joined the NL East). The Marlins were owned by H. Wayne Huizenga, who had made his fortune in the entertainment industry.

In their first season, the Marlins won 64 games. Reliever Bryan Harvey managed to **save** 45 of those wins, third best in the NL. Florida finished sixth in the new seven-team division, ahead of the last-place Mets.

The Marlins finished last in the strike-shortened season of 1994 and fourth in 1995. In '95, though, several young players blossomed, giving Florida fans hope for the future. Pitcher Pat Rapp posted a 14–7 mark, while rookie second baseman Quilvio Veras led the league with 56 stolen bases.

In 1996, the Marlins won 80 games to finish third in the East. Many bright spots emerged on the field. Outfielder Gary Sheffield smacked 42 homers. Lefty

The south Florida
area gave notice
it was ready for
a big-league
franchise in 1991.
A spring-training
record 67,654 fans
watched the Orioles
and Yankees play a
game at Pro Player
Stadium (then called
Joe Robbie Stadium)
in March that year.

The Marlins' first
draft pick was
former University of
Miami star catcher
Charles Johnson.
He eventually
played a key role
on Florida's first
championship team.

Al Leiter struck out 200 batters. Righty Kevin Brown posted a league-leading 1.89 earned run average (ERA). And reliever Robb Nen racked up 35 saves.

The Marlins' off-season following the 1996 season was one of the busiest in baseball history. First, the four-year-old club signed veteran manager Jim Leyland to manage the team. Then, within a three-week period, the Marlins signed six **free agents,** practically creating a whole new team. Moises Alou, Bobby Bonilla, John Cangelosi, Dennis Cook, Jim Eisenreich, and Alex Fernandez joined Sheffield, Brown, Leiter, second-year shortstop Edgar Renteria, and rookie pitcher Livan Hernandez. Overnight, they formed one of the best teams in the league.

The Marlins fought the Atlanta Braves for the NL East title all through the 1997 season. Although the Braves took the division, the Marlins qualified for the postseason as the NL **wild-card** team. In the Division Series, the Marlins swept the Giants, then stunned the Braves, beating them in the NLCS in six games.

Livan Hernandez, who had defected from Cuba, was named the Most Valuable Player (MVP) of the NLCS. He went on to repeat that honor in the World Series, as well, as the Marlins beat the Cleveland

When Craig Counsell (30) crossed home plate with the winning run in
Game 7 of the 1997 World Series, the Marlins were baseball's champions.

The Marlins' first manager was Rene Lachemann. Rene's older brother, Marcel, was the club's first pitching coach.

The Miami area has long been a hot spot for the game of baseball. Many major league teams train there in the spring. Florida got its first minor league team in 1912, when the Miami Magicians entered the Class D East Florida State League.

Indians in seven games. Not only were the Marlins the first wild-card team to win the World Series, but they also did it faster than any other **expansion team** in history. They took the title in only their fifth year.

Just as quickly as that great team had been built, it was broken apart. Following the incredible 1997 season, Huizenga claimed that he had lost huge amounts of money on the team. He immediately began getting rid of his best players. Then he sold the team to businessman John Henry. For the next two seasons, the Marlins finished in last place.

Some players showed promise, however. In 2000, pitcher Ryan Dempster won 14 games and was selected to the All-Star team. Antonio Alfonseca led the majors with 45 saves. Luis Castillo led the majors with 62 stolen bases and batted .334 leading off. Veterans Cliff Floyd and Mike Lowell both returned to form, as the Marlins climbed out of the cellar, finishing third.

Two fourth-place finishes preceded a magical season in 2003. After the club got off to a slow start, 72-year-old Jack McKeon replaced Jeff Torborg as the club's manager. Rookie left-hander Dontrelle Willis came up from the minors and confused NL hitters with his unusual pitching motion. The

Third baseman Mike Lowell was a key player for Florida's 2003 champion team.

Marlins had the best record in the league over the last four months of the regular season to earn a wild-card berth. Then, after beating the Giants and Cubs in the playoffs, Florida upset the New York Yankees in six games to win the World Series. Josh Beckett,

Florida's Kevin Brown pitched a no-hitter **against the San Francisco Giants on June 10, 1997. The Marlins won the game 9–0.**

a 23-year-old pitcher with unlimited potential, shut
down the Yankees on five hits in the final game to
secure the Marlins' second title in their brief history.

Young pitcher Josh Beckett won the decisive game of the 2003 World Series.

The New York Mets

Following the 1957 season, the Dodgers left Brooklyn for Los Angeles and the Giants left New York for San Francisco. New York City, the center of the baseball universe for most of the 1950s, was left without an NL team.

In 1962, the NL expanded to 10 teams, and the Mets were born. Former Yankees manager Casey Stengel, one of baseball's most colorful and beloved figures, was brought in to manage the new club. Former Brooklyn Dodgers stars Roger Craig and Gil Hodges joined the team.

The Mets were terrible during their first season. They lost 120 games that year, the most by a major league team in the 20th century.

Amazingly, New York fans—thrilled to have an NL club back in town—took to this group of lovable losers. Over their first three years, the last-place Mets drew more fans in New York than the pennant-winning Yankees.

In 1964, the Mets moved from the Polo

The Mets' fortunes began to turn when Tom Seaver first arrived in 1967.

Grounds—the former home of the New York Giants—
into brand-new Shea Stadium. Despite continued
dismal play, signs of hope were emerging by 1967.
Mostly they were in the form of rookie pitcher Tom
Seaver, who won 16 games, and new manager Gil
Hodges. The next year, the Mets added lefty pitcher
Jerry Koosman, who won 19 games. The club got
out of last place with its first 70-plus win season.

In 1969, the first year of divisional play, the Mets
got off to a slow start. But by early summer, they

The "Miracle Mets" stunned Baltimore in five games to win the 1969 World Series.

were winning consistently. Future Hall of Famer Seaver had his best year, going 25–7 and winning the first of his three Cy Young Awards. The Mets won the NL East, then swept the Atlanta Braves in the first NLCS.

The "Miracle Mets," as the '69 team came to be known, then pulled off a stunning upset of the Baltimore Orioles in the World Series. In eight years, the Mets had gone from lovable losers to world champs.

The Mets' uniform colors were taken from the Dodgers (blue) and the Giants (orange and black), the two teams that left New York following the 1957 season.

Just before the start of the 1972 season, Gil
Hodges suffered a fatal heart attack. He was replaced
by Yankees legend and Mets coach Yogi Berra. In
1973, the Mets won the NL East for the second time
in the closest race of the 20th century. They beat
Cincinnati to win their second pennant but lost to
Oakland in the World Series.

The next 10 years were terrible for the team.
In 1980, Frank Cashen, who had built the Orioles

Right-hander Dwight Gooden overpowered hitters with his blazing fastball.

into a powerhouse in the late 1960s, was brought in as general manager.

Over the next few years, a combination of players from the farm system and some shrewd trades brought the Mets back into contention. In 1983, rookie slugger Darryl Strawberry arrived, and veteran first baseman Keith Hernandez came over from the Cardinals. The following year brought a new manager (former Oriole Davey Johnson), two rookie pitchers (Ron Darling and Dwight Gooden), and a second-place finish.

In 1985, catcher Gary Carter came over from the Expos. Gooden, at age 20, won the Cy Young Award with an astounding 24–4 record and an ERA of 1.53. The team again finished second, this time winning 98 games.

In 1986, it all came together for the Mets. The team cruised to first place in the NL East with 108 victories. The postseason proved more difficult. The Mets won the NL pennant in a hard-fought series against Houston, including an epic 16-inning Game 6 at the Astrodome. Then, one strike away from losing to the Red Sox in Game 6 of the World Series, the Mets rallied. They won the game, then the series, for their second championship.

The Mets' first manager, Casey Stengel, was known for his often baffling, always amusing way of expressing himself. He sometimes used a "language" that came to be known as *Stengelese*. For instance, upon his retirement in 1965, Stengel summed up his career by saying, "There comes a time in every man's life, and I've had plenty of them."

The Mets returned to the postseason in 1988 with the same core of the '86 championship team, plus pitcher David Cone. Cone's 20–3 record and 2.22 ERA led the staff. In the NLCS, the Mets lost to the underachieving Los Angeles Dodgers.

The early 1990s were a down period for the team. In 1996, Bobby Valentine took over as manager. In 1998, the Mets acquired pitcher Al Leiter and catcher Mike Piazza. Leiter would win 17 games for the Mets in '98, and Piazza became the best offensive player the Mets have ever had.

In 1999, the Mets returned to the postseason via the wild card. After beating Arizona in the Division Series, they lost to Atlanta in the NLCS. The following year, the Mets again won the wild card. This time, they beat the Giants in the Division Series and the Cardinals in the NLCS to win their first pennant since 1986.

Their opponents in the 2000 World Series were the New York Yankees, setting up a "Subway Series" reminiscent of the classic Yankees-Dodgers and Yankees-Giants World Series of the 1950s. The Yankees beat their crosstown rivals in five games.

The Mets' Mike Piazza is arguably the greatest hitting catcher in big-league history.

Tom Seaver originally was signed out of the University of Southern California (USC) in 1966 by the Atlanta Braves. When baseball officials terminated the contract, the Mets, Phillies, and Cleveland Indians chose to match the Braves' offer. The names of the three teams were put in a hat. The Mets' name was drawn, and they got their ace pitcher!

New York has high hopes for youngsters such as third baseman David Wright.

Following their appearance in the 2000 World Series, the Mets suffered through several disappointing years. High-priced but under-performing free agents led to losing records each season from 2002 through 2004.

The Philadelphia Phillies

Of the five teams currently playing in the NL East, the Phillies have been playing in the same city, under the same team name, for the longest time (since 1890). The team joined the NL in 1883, playing under the nickname "the Quakers."

The team's early years boasted an outfield made up of three future Hall of Famers—Ed Delahanty, Billy Hamilton, and Sam Thompson. In 1894, the team batting average was .349, still the highest for any team in major league history.

Between 1899 and 1910, the Phillies suffered losing seasons. The next ray of hope came in 1911 in the form of rookie pitcher Grover Cleveland Alexander. The future Hall of Famer, who would go on to win 373

ED DELAHANTY
ONE OF THE GAME'S GREATEST SLUGGER
LED NATIONAL LEAGUE HITTERS IN
1899 WITH AN AVERAGE OF .408 FOR
PHILADELPHIA; AMERICAN LEAGUE
BATTERS IN 1902 WITH A MARK OF .37
FOR WASHINGTON. MADE 6 HITS IN 6
TIMES AT BAT TWICE DURING CAREE
AND ONCE HIT 4 HOME RUNS ...

Hall of Famer Robin Roberts won 20 or more games for the Phillies for six consecutive years from 1950 to 1955.

career games, kept the Phillies in the pennant race for most of the season.

In 1915, Alexander posted a league-leading and career-best ERA of 1.22, helping the Phillies to their first pennant. After winning the World Series opener, the Phillies lost four in a row to the Boston Red Sox to lose the series.

After Alexander won 30 games in 1917 (the team finished second), the club traded him to Chicago. The next 30 or so years were dark ones for the Phillies.

In the late 1940s, the featured players were

Richie Ashburn shows how to dive headfirst in this magazine shoot.

the "Whiz Kids"—Dick Sisler, Richie Ashburn, Curt Simmons, and Robin Roberts. They formed the core center of the team. The Whiz Kids won Philadelphia's second pennant in 1950 but were frustrated in the World Series, getting swept by the Yankees in four straight games.

Roberts starred for the team over the next few years as a starting pitcher, winning 20 or more for six seasons in a row, but the Phillies always fell short. By the end of the 1950s, they had plunged to the NL cellar. In 1961, they lost 23 straight games, the longest losing streak in the 20th century.

In 1964, pitcher Jim Bunning and slugger Richie Allen led the Phillies to a big lead in August. But 10 straight late-September losses helped blow the pennant.

The 1970s brought the arrival of arguably the greatest pitcher and greatest hitter the Phillies have ever had. In 1972, they got lefty Steve Carlton from St. Louis. He won 27 games that year for the last-place team, capturing his first Cy Young Award. In 1974, second-year third baseman Mike Schmidt

Lefty Steve Carlton won four Cy Young Awards between 1962 and 1972.

Hall of Famer Jim Bunning is one of only 17 pitchers ever to throw a perfect game. The father of nine children did it on Father's Day in 1964! He went on to become a U.S. senator in his post-playing career.

On June 23, 1971, Philadelphia's Rick Wise no-hit the Cincinnati Reds 4–0. He was the hitting star that day, too, blasting two home runs!

Hall of Fame third baseman Mike Schmidt not only was a mighty slugger, but he also was an exceptional fielder. His 10 career Gold Glove Awards rank second only to the great Brooks Robinson.

Mike Schmidt is the greatest slugger in Phillies history.

blossomed into one of the league's premier power hitters. Together, they would lead the Phillies into the finest years in the club's long history.

In 1976, the team had its best regular season ever, winning 101 games and the NL East. They won the division again the following year. In 1978, they won their third straight East title, but lost for the third straight time in the NLCS. Dallas Green took over as manager in 1979, and veteran Pete Rose joined the team that year.

In 1980, it all came together for the Phillies. They captured the NL East, led by Schmidt, who was the league's MVP, and Carlton, who won his third Cy Young Award. The Phillies beat Houston in the NLCS to capture their first pennant in 30 years. Then they beat Kansas City in six games to win their first and only World Series.

In 1982, the Phillies finished second. Carlton, though, won another Cy Young Award, becoming the first pitcher ever to win the award four times. The following year, the Phillies won their fourth NL pennant, but lost the World Series to Baltimore.

But the Phillies' golden years were about to end. Schmidt retired with 548 home runs. Carlton, who eventually played for several big-league teams near the end of his career, retired in 1988 with 4,136 strikeouts, second all-time only to Nolan Ryan.

The Phillies won their fifth pennant in 1993, beating Atlanta in the NLCS, but lost to Toronto in

In 2001, outfielder Bobby Abreu became the Phillies' first player to join the 30–30 club (30 home runs and 30 steals in the same season).

Current star Bobby Abreu combines speed with power
to be one of the best outfielders in the league.

Tug McGraw was the
Phillies' relief ace at
the 1980 World Series.
Tug's son is Tim
McGraw, the country
music superstar.

the World Series. The 1990s saw the rise of pitching
star Curt Schilling, who struck out 300 batters in
1997 and '98, and hitting stars Mike Lieberthal and
Bobby Abreu.

Led by Abreu and slugging first baseman Jim
Thome, the team has regained its competitive edge
in the new millennium.

The Washington Nationals

Washington, D.C.'s team began life in 1969 as the Montreal Expos amid a flurry of hope, national pride, and excellent attendance. That year, the NL split into the East and West divisions. Two new teams were added, the San Diego Padres in the West and the Expos in the East.

The Expos were named after Expo '67, the World's Fair held in Montreal. In their first season, the team compiled a 52–110 record, finishing last in the NL East. But they outdrew the new Padres club by more than double, attracting more than 1.2 million fans.

In 1971, the Expos moved out of the NL East cellar, finishing fifth in the six-team division. They repeated that finish in 1972.

The following year, the team's first two stars emerged. Ken Singleton drove in 103 runs. Rookie pitcher Steve Rogers put together a 1.54 ERA. Reliever Mike Marshall set a major league record with 92 appear-

ances, saving a league-leading 31 games. The NL East race that season was the tightest of the 20th century, with all six teams, including the young Expos, in the race well into September. They finished fourth, only $3^1/_2$ games behind the division-champion Mets.

By 1975, the Expos had sunk back to last place, where they remained in 1976. The next year, the team moved from Jarry Park into brand-new Olympic Stadium, which had been built for the 1976 Summer Olympics.

Dick Williams took over as manager in 1977. The team added veteran slugger Tony Perez, rookie Andre Dawson, and catcher Gary Carter. (Perez and Carter eventually were **inducted** in baseball's Hall of Fame.)

The 1980 season saw the Expos in first place heading into the final series of the year. The Phillies took two of three from Montreal in that series to edge out the Expos for the division title.

In the split season (due to a players' strike) of 1981, Montreal won the NL East in the second half of the year. The Expos captured their first NL East crown by beating Philadelphia in a special playoff.

The Expos franchise was less than two weeks old when Bill Stoneman recorded its first no-hitter. He beat the Phillies 7–0 on April 17, 1969.

Andre Dawson was a talented star who could hit, run, field, and throw.

The Expos moved into Olympic Stadium in 1977. The site also has hosted rock concerts, a visit from Pope John Paul II, and five Grey Cup games (the "Super Bowl" of Canadian football). In 1987, the stadium's dome was added. Two years later, the dome was made retractable, meaning it can be mechanically pulled back.

But they lost to the Dodgers in the NLCS.

In 1988 and '89, the Expos got off to fast starts, spending time in first place in the NL East, before slumping to .500 finishes (81–81) in each season.

Under new manager Felipe Alou, the Expos climbed from fifth place to second in 1992. They were led by pitchers Ken Hill and Dennis Martinez,

Hall of Fame catcher Gary Carter played 12 of his 19 big-league seasons in Montreal.

Dennis Martinez tossed a perfect game against the Dodgers in 1991.

and outfielder Larry Walker, who went on to become one of the game's best hitters. In 1993, the team again finished second, compiling an impressive 94–68 record.

On August 7, 1994, the Expos were not only in first place in the NL East, but they also had the best record in major league baseball. A postseason appearance seemed certain. Then, less than a week later, the players went on strike, and the rest of the season—and the postseason—was canceled.

In 1995, the Expos dropped into last place. The gulf between the wealthy big-market teams and the smaller-market clubs, which could not compete for expensive free agents, was beginning to hurt the

Superstar outfielder Vladimir Guerrero was only 17 years old when the Expos signed him to a contract in 1993.

While playing for Montreal in 1997, Pedro Martinez
won the first of his three Cy Young Awards.

Frank Robinson took
over as the Expos'
manager in 2002.
The Hall of Fame
outfielder's first
managerial job came
while he was still a
player for Cleveland
in 1975. He was
the first African
American manager
in the major leagues.

Expos. In 1997, Pedro Martinez became the first
Expos pitcher to win the Cy Young Award. But the
team could not afford to keep Martinez, as well as
some of their top offensive players.

In 1998, two young stars emerged. Power-hit-
ting outfielder Vladimir Guerrero and closer Ugueth
Urbina led the club to a fourth-place finish. New
ownership in 1999 didn't help the Expos' financial
difficulties. Things got worse in 2000, despite the
fact that Guerrero broke his own team records with
a .345 batting average and 44 homers.

In 2002, the club was on the verge of being
dissolved and its players split up in a draft. The
Major League Baseball organization took over owner-

ship of the Expos. Young Omar Minaya, who had had great success as the Mets' assistant general manager, became the Expos' general manager. Hall of Fame slugger and veteran manager Frank Robinson was named the team's skipper. In 2003, the Expos played 22 "home" games at Hiram Bithorn Stadium in San Juan, Puerto Rico.

Finally, the club's uncertain future was resolved late in 2004, when it was announced that the franchise would move to Washington, D.C., in time for the 2005 season.

The Expos originally played their home games in Jarry Park. It was a 3,000-seat city park that was expanded to seat 28,500 in time for the 1969 season opener.

Second baseman Jose Vidro (making the tag) has been one of the Expos' most consistent stars since breaking into the lineup full-time in 1999.

Stat Stuff

TEAM RECORDS (THROUGH 2004)

Team	All-time Record	World Series Titles (Most Recent)	Number of Times in the Postseason	Top Manager (Wins)
Atlanta*	9,668–9,544	3 (1995)	19	Bobby Cox (2,002)
Florida	880–997	2 (2003)	2	Rene Lachemann (221)
New York Mets	3,228–3,598	2 (1986)	6	Davey Johnson (595)
Philadelphia	8,680–9,964	1 (1980)	9	Gene Mauch (646)
Washington, D.C.**	2,755–2,943	0	1	Felipe Alou (691)

*includes Boston and Milwaukee
**includes Montreal

NATIONAL LEAGUE EAST
CAREER LEADERS (THROUGH 2004)

Atlanta

Category	Name (Years with Team)	Total
Batting Average	Hugh Duffy (1891–1900)	.332
Home Runs	Hank Aaron (1954–1974)	733
RBI	Hank Aaron (1954–1974)	2,202
Stolen Bases	Herman Long (1890–1902)	433
Wins	Warren Spahn (1942, 1946–1964)	356
Saves	John Smoltz (1988–2004)	154
Strikeouts	Phil Niekro (1964–1983, 1987)	2,912

NATIONAL LEAGUE EAST CAREER LEADERS (THROUGH 2004)

Florida

Category	Name (Years with Team)	Total
Batting Average	Juan Pierre (2003–04)	.316
Home Runs	Mike Lowell (1999–2004)	135
RBI	Jeff Conine (1993–97, 2003–04)	520
	Mike Lowell (1999–2004)	520
Stolen Bases	Luis Castillo (1996–2004)	271
Wins	Brad Penny (2000–04)	48
Saves	Robb Nen (1993–97)	108
Strikeouts	Ryan Dempster (1998–2002)	628

New York

Category	Name (Years with Team)	Total
Batting Average	John Olerud (1997–99)	.315
Home Runs	Darryl Strawberry (1983–1990)	252
RBI	Darryl Strawberry (1983–1990)	733
Stolen Bases	Mookie Wilson (1980–89)	281
Wins	Tom Seaver (1967–1977, 1983)	198
Saves	John Franco (1990–2004)	276
Strikeouts	Tom Seaver (1967–1977, 1983)	2,541

NATIONAL LEAGUE EAST CAREER LEADERS (THROUGH 2004)

Philadelphia

Category	Name (Years with Team)	Total
Batting Average	Billy Hamilton (1890–95)	.361
Home Runs	Mike Schmidt (1972–1989)	548
RBI	Mike Schmidt (1972–1989)	1,595
Stolen Bases	Billy Hamilton (1890–95)	508
Wins	Steve Carlton (1972–1986)	241
Saves	Jose Mesa (2001–03)	111
Strikeouts	Steve Carlton (1972–1986)	3,031

Washington, D.C.

Category	Name (Years with Team)	Total
Batting Average	Vladimir Guerrero (1996–2003)	.323
Home Runs	Vladimir Guerrero (1996–2003)	234
RBI	Tim Wallach (1980–1992)	905
Stolen Bases	Tim Raines (1979–1990, 2001)	635
Wins	Steve Rogers (1973–1985)	158
Saves	Jeff Reardon (1981–86)	152
Strikeouts	Steve Rogers (1973–1985)	1,621

Glossary

aces—the best pitchers on a team

cellar—last place

closers—relief pitchers brought in at the end of games to save their victories

Cy Young Award—the award annually given to the best pitcher in each league

expansion team—a new franchise that starts from scratch, thus increasing (or expanding) the total number of clubs in a given league

free agents—players who have completed their contracts with one team and are free to sign with any other team

inducted—to be brought into, or included with, membership

Negro Leagues—baseball leagues that existed from the 1920s through the 1950s; they were composed of African American players, who were barred until 1947 from playing in the major leagues

no-hitter—a complete game in which the pitcher or pitchers for one team do not allow the opposing team any hits

pennants—the championships of each league (American and National)

postseason—the playoffs, which start with the Division Series, continue with the League Championship Series, and conclude with the World Series

save—the action of a relief pitcher in successfully protecting a team's lead

veteran—a player who has been in the game for many years

wild card—a team that finishes in second place in its division but still makes the playoffs

World Series—baseball's championship event; the winners of the AL and the NL pennants annually meet in a best-of-seven series to determine the world champion

Time Line

1876   The Braves franchise becomes a charter member of the newly formed National League.

1883   The Phillies franchise debuts in Philadelphia; the club is known as "the Quakers."

1953   The Braves move from Boston to Milwaukee.

1962   The New York Mets debut but lose a record 120 games.

1966   The Braves move from Milwaukee to Atlanta.

1969   Baseball expands to Canada for the first time when Montreal debuts as an expansion team.

   The "Miracle Mets" win their first World Series in only their eighth season.

1980   In their 98th season, the Phillies win the World Series for the first time.

1993   The Florida Marlins join the NL as an expansion team.

1995   The Braves win their third World Series, their first in Atlanta.

1997   In only their fifth season, the Marlins earn a wild-card playoff berth and go on to win the World Series.

2003   The surprising Marlins win the World Series for the second time in their brief history.

2005   The Expos franchise moves from Montreal to Washington, D.C.

For More Information

BOOKS

Dewey, Donald, and Nicholas Acocella. *The Encyclopedia of Major League Teams.* New York: HarperCollins, 1993.

Golenbock, Peter. *Amazin': The Miraculous History of New York's Most Beloved Baseball Team.* New York: Saint Martin's Press, 2002.

Jordan, David M. *Occasional Glory: The History of the Philadelphia Phillies.* Jefferson, N.C.: McFarland & Company, 2002.

Nichols, John. *The History of the Florida Marlins.* Mankato, Minn.: Creative Education, 1999.

Stewart, Wayne. *The History of the Atlanta Braves.* Mankato, Minn.: Creative Education, 2003.

ON THE WEB

Visit our home page for lots of links about the National League East teams: *http://www.childsworld.com/links.html*

Note to Parents, Teachers, and Librarians: We routinely check our Web links to make sure they're safe, active sites—so encourage your readers to check them out!

Index

ABOUT THE AUTHOR

Michael Teitelbaum has been a writer and editor of children's books and magazines for more than 20 years. Michael (a lifelong fan of the New York Mets and the New York Knicks) and his wife, Sheleigah, split their time between New York City and their 160-year-old farmhouse in the Catskill Mountains of upstate New York.